Little
Science
Stars

Forces and Motion

The Best Start in Science

By Clint Twist

ticktock

ISBN-13: 978 1 84898 060 0 pbk
This revised edition published in 2009 by *ticktock* Media Ltd

Printed in China
9 8 7 6 5 4 3 2 1

Copyright © *ticktock* Entertainment Ltd 2005
First published in Great Britain as *Check It Out!* in 2005 by *ticktock* Media Ltd,
The Old Sawmill, 103 Goods Station Road, Tunbridge Wells, Kent, TN1 2DP

Picture credits (t=top, b=bottom, c=centre, l=left, r=right,
OFC=outside front cover, OBC=outside back cover):

Corbis: 7t, 15tl, 15b, 16t, 17c, 17b. Powerstock: 7b, 9t, 9c, 11t, 11c, 12t, 14t,
18 all, 20c, 21t, 21bl. Shutterstock: OFC, 1 all, 3 all 4–5 all, 6 all, 8 all, 9b,
10 all, 11bl, 12c, 12b, 13 all, 14b both, 14–15 (background), 15r, 16br, 17t,
19 all, 20t, 20b, 21br, 22–23 all, OBC both.

Every effort has been made to trace the copyright holders and we apologize in
advance for any unintentional omissions. We would be pleased to insert the
appropriate acknowledgements in any subsequent edition of this publication.

Contents

Any words appearing in the text in bold, **like this**, are explained in the Glossary.

Forces are all around us,
making things move.
How many moving things
can you spot today?

Push

Shape change

Pull

Forces are at work every
day in our world.
Let's find out what forces
can do!

What is motion?

We move around all day long!

Sometimes we run.

Sometimes we ride a bike.

Sometimes we travel in a car or on a bus or train.

When we move from one **position** to another, we are in **motion**.

6

This tiger is in motion. He is walking across the snow.

The opposite of motion is **stillness**.

The tiger sits down beside the trees. Now he is still.

Things that are not moving are not in motion. Their positions do not change.

What is a force?

Things do not move on their own. They need a force to make them move. **Pushing** is a kind of force.

This man is moving the lawnmower using a pushing force.

The girl is in motion on the swing. The boy is pushing her!

This family is using a pushing force to move the trolley. They move it from one position to another.

This cat is pushing against the trolley. She is using force to make the trolley move.

Force

With two cats, there is more force pushing against the trolley.

More force

Do you think two cats will move the trolley more or less than one cat?

9

What is a pull?

A pull is another type of force.

This girl uses a **pulling** force to move the suitcase.

Plough

These horses are using a pulling force to move the plough through the soil.

Trailer

Truck

This trailer is in motion. The truck is using a pulling force to move it.

This dog is pulling on the rope toy.

It is easy to move a **light** or small **load**. The dog can easily pull one small rabbit.

Now the load is heavier.

Will the dog have to use more or less force to pull a whole family of rabbits?

11

Push or pull?

Everything needs a push or a pull to make it move!

Can you say whether these actions are pushes or pulls?

1 This boy rolls some marbles. PUSH or PULL?

2 This boy skates on his skateboard. PUSH OR PULL?

3 This boy puts on his helmet. PUSH or PULL?

4 This girl opens her umbrella. PUSH or PULL?

5 This girl zips her jacket. PUSH OR PULL?

6 This boy kicks his ball. PUSH OR PULL?

Answers

6)	PUSH
5)	PULL
4)	PUSH
3)	PULL
2)	PUSH
1)	PUSH

13

How do we use force?

A gentle push, or small amount of force, will make the toy car move slowly.

A lot of force, will make it move fast.

We can use force to stop a moving object.

A toy car is small and light. We can use our hands to stop it moving.

A real car is large, heavy and dangerous. We could not use force from our hands to stop a real car.

The goalkeeper applies force with his hands to stop the ball.

The footballer uses force from his foot to stop the ball.

We can use force to make a moving object change its direction.

Look at the arrows. The force from the boy's racket will change the ball's direction.

How do things move on slopes?

Slopes have an effect on the way things move along them.

This bear is **sliding** down a slope covered in snow.

The steeper the slope, the faster the bear slides.

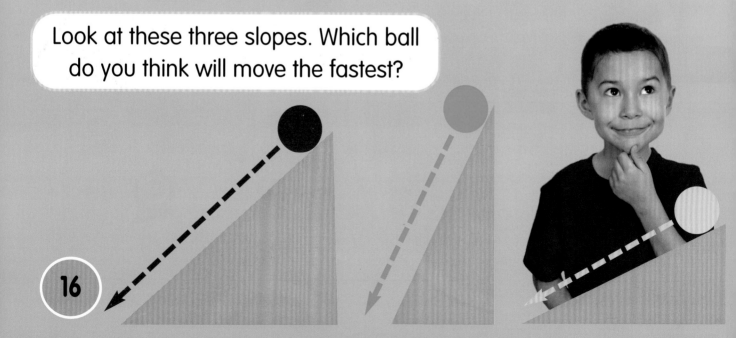

Look at these three slopes. Which ball do you think will move the fastest?

The snowboarder moves
fast down a slope.

The snowboard slides
over the snow.

These dogs are pulling
a sledge that slides
over the snow.

The dogs are pulling
the sledge up a slope.

It's harder to move up a
slope than it is to move
down a slope.

What is friction?

Friction is a force that stops things from moving easily.

There is friction when one thing slides against another.

Snow has a **smooth** surface with little friction, so things slide easily.

Grass has a **rough** surface. There is a lot more friction.

It is more difficult to slide down a grass slope than a snow slope.

Different surfaces have more or less friction than one another.

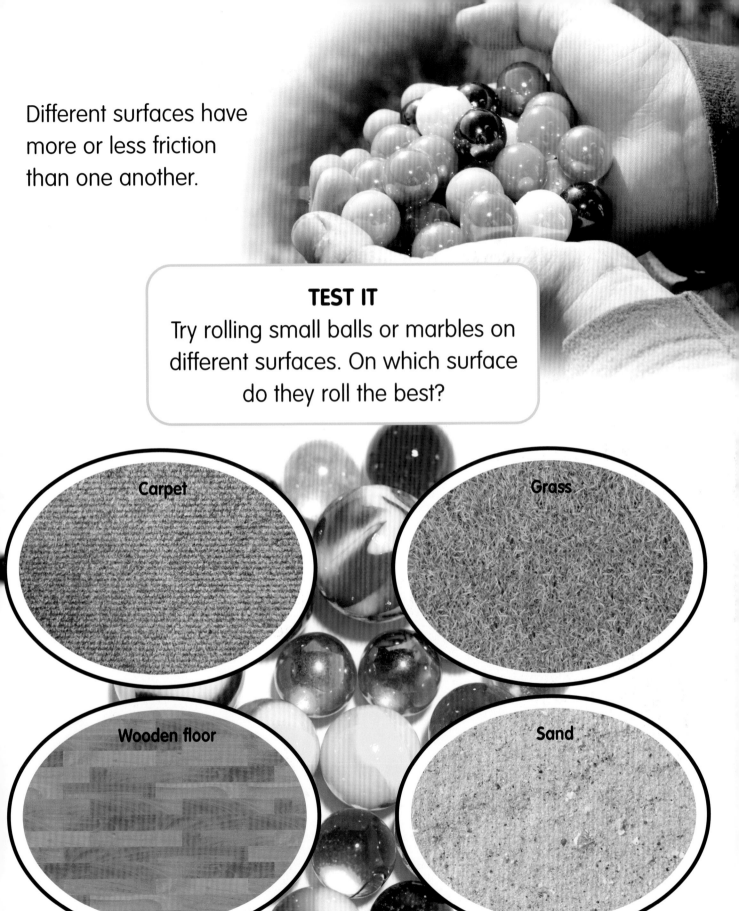

TEST IT
Try rolling small balls or marbles on different surfaces. On which surface do they roll the best?

Carpet

Grass

Wooden floor

Sand

Can force change the shape of an object?

Force doesn't just make things move. Force can also change the shape of some objects.

Rubber ball

When working with **dough**, you use force to push and pull the dough into shapes with your hands.

Force from the rolling pin makes the dough flat.

You can see
force in action
on modelling clay.

Push your finger against a
piece of modelling clay and
make a small dent.

Dent

If you push with more force,
the dent will get bigger.

Questions and answers

Q What tummy-flipping theme park ride has lots of up and down slopes?

A A rollercoaster!

Q How many different ways can you think of to move from one place to another?

A Here are some ideas:
Skip
Hop
Roll
Run

Q What type of force do we use to open a car door?

A A pull force.

Q Do you think ice skates have more or less friction on ice than trainers?

A Ice skates have smooth blades on the bottom so they have less friction.

Q Do you think hitting a nail with a hammer is a push or a pull force?

A It's a push force.

Q Do we use a push or a pull force to open a bag of crisps?

A A pull force.

Q Do we use a push or a pull force when we jump?

A A push force.

Glossary

Dough A mixture of flour and water that can be baked into bread or pizza.

Forces Things that cause movement, such as a pull or push.

Friction A force that slows down movement.

Light Something that does not weigh very much. It is the opposite of heavy.

Load Something that is moved from one place to another.

Motion Another word for movement.

Position The place where one object is in relation to other objects.

Pulling A force that is applied from in front of an object to be moved.

Pushing A force that is applied from behind the object to be moved.

Rough A surface with many bumps.

Sliding A movement that takes place when two surfaces are touching each other.

Slopes Surfaces or lines with one end either higher or lower than the other.

Smooth A surface that has no bumps.

Stillness When nothing is moving.

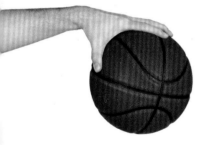

Index